HOLLY JOLLY CHRISTMAS

FIVE 5 FINGER PIANO

CONTENTS

ISBN 0-634-00855-2

HAL•LEONARD®
CORPORATION
7777 W. BLUEMOUND RD. P.O. BOX 13819 MILWAUKEE, WI 53213

Visit Hal Leonard Online at
www.halleonard.com

Frosty the Snow Man

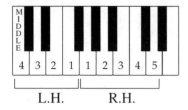

Words and Music by Steve Nelson
and Jack Rollins

With a bounce

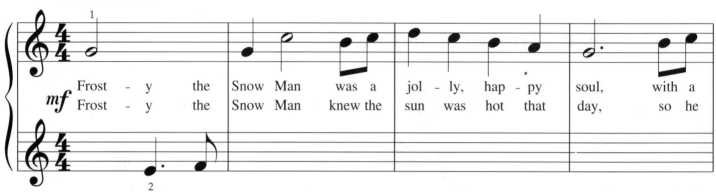

Frost - y   the   Snow Man   was a   jol - ly,   hap - py   soul,   with a
Frost - y   the   Snow Man   knew the sun was   hot that   day,   so he

corn cob pipe and a   but - ton nose and two   eyes made out   of   coal.
said, "Let's run and we'll have some fun   now be - fore   I   melt a - way."

Duet Part (Student plays one octave higher than written.)

With a bounce

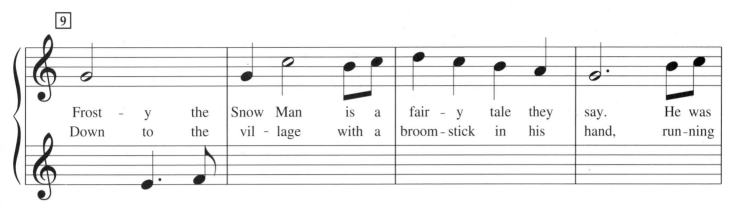

Frost - y the Snow Man is a fair - y tale they say. He was
Down to the vil - lage with a broom - stick in his hand, run - ning

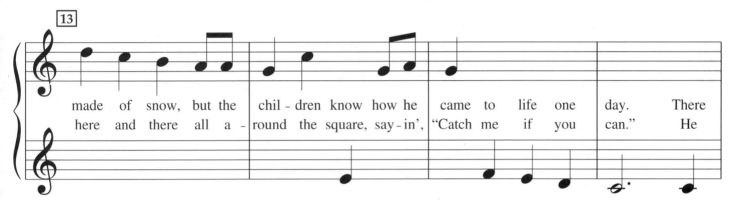

made of snow, but the chil - dren know how he came to life one day. There
here and there all a - round the square, say - in', "Catch me if you can." He

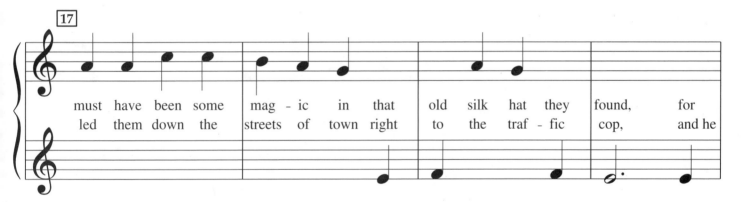

must have been some mag - ic in that old silk hat they found, for
led them down the streets of town right to the traf - fic cop, and he

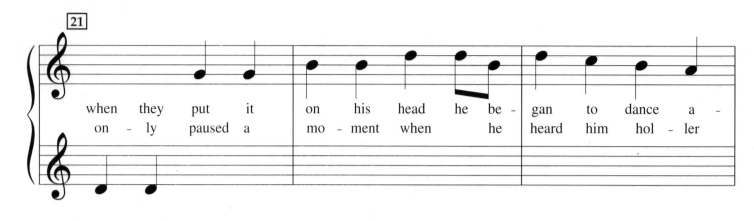

when they put it on his head he be-gan to dance a-

on - ly paused a mo - ment when he heard him hol - ler

round. Oh, Frost - y the Snow Man was a - live as he could

"Stop!" For Frost - y the Snow Man had to hur - ry on his

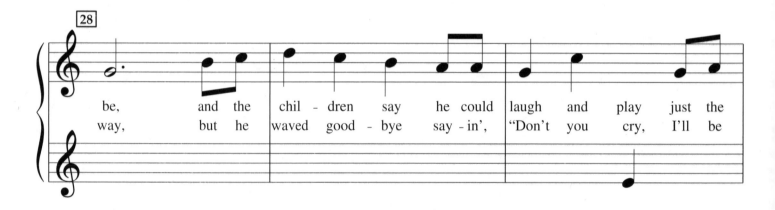

be, and the chil - dren say he could laugh and play just the

way, but he waved good - bye say - in', "Don't you cry, I'll be

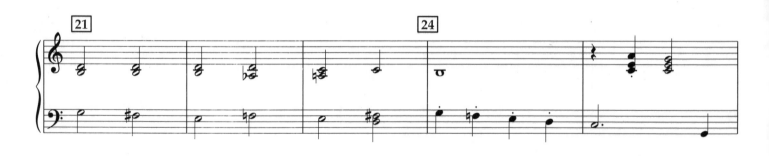

A Holly Jolly Christmas

Music and Lyrics by
Johnny Marks

Duet Part (Student plays one octave higher than written.)

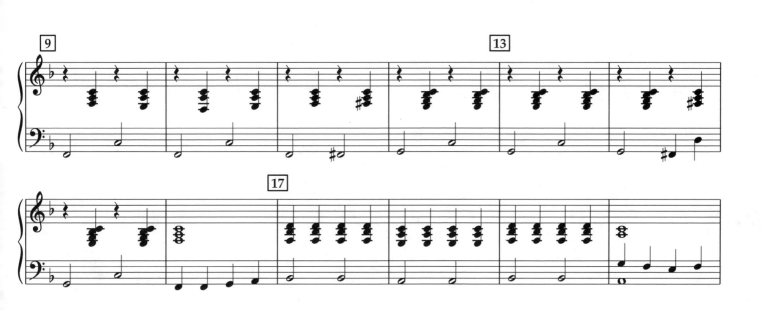

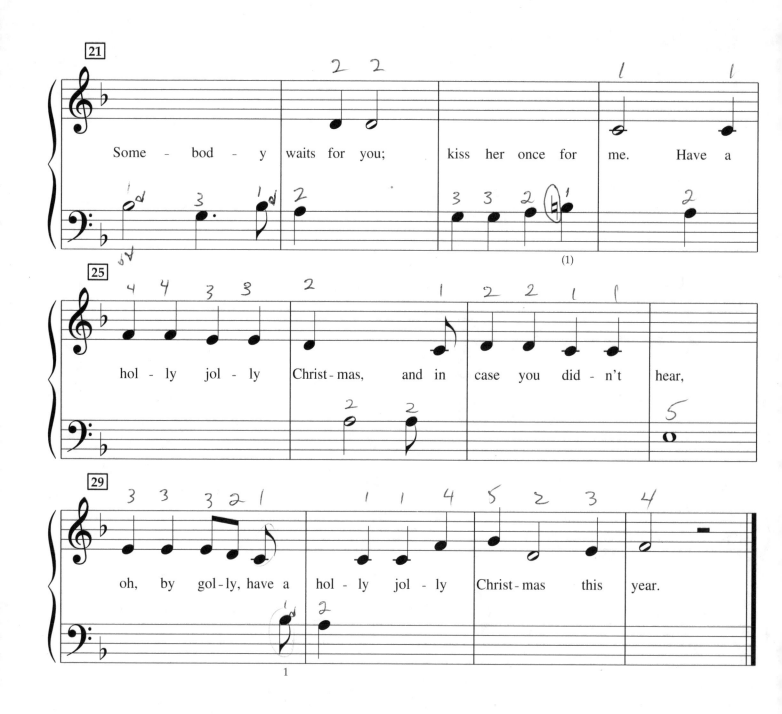

I'll Be Home for Christmas

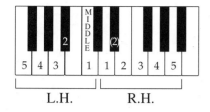

Words and Music by Kim Gannon
and Walter Kent

Moderately, with feeling

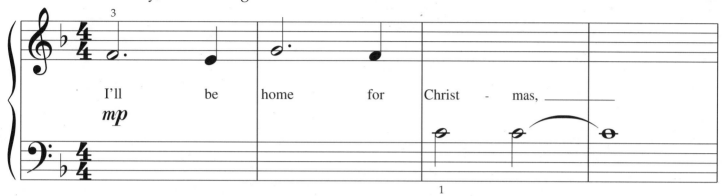

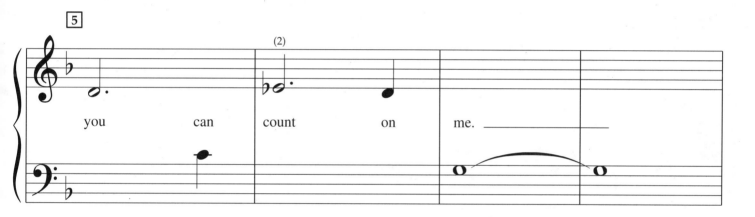

Duet Part (Student plays one octave higher than written.)

Moderately, with feeling

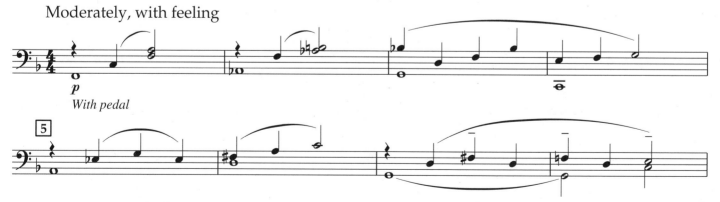

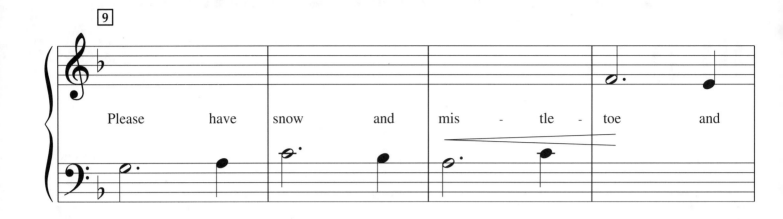

Please have snow and mis - tle - toe and

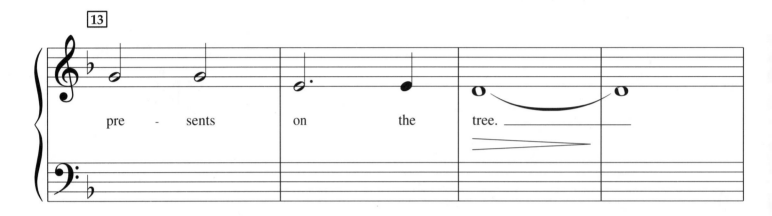

pre - sents on the tree. _____

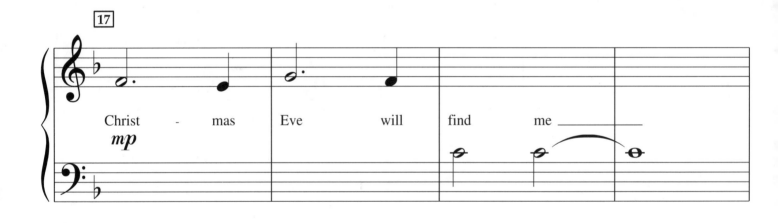

Christ - mas Eve will find me _____

mp

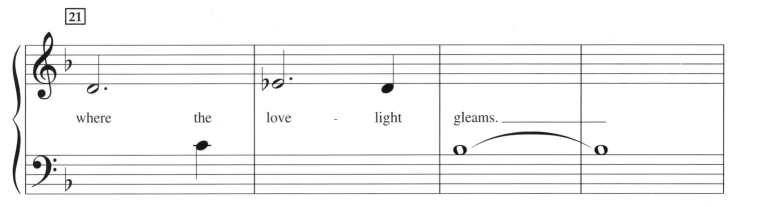

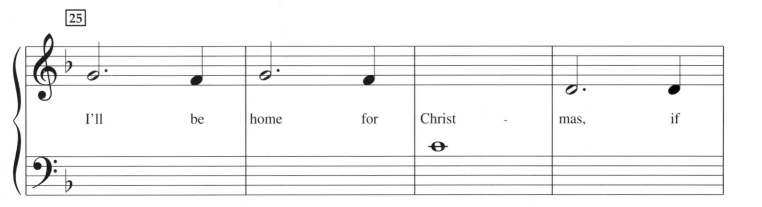

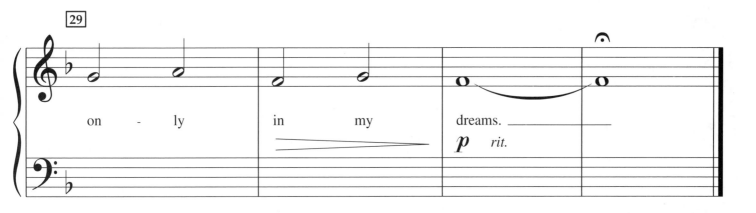

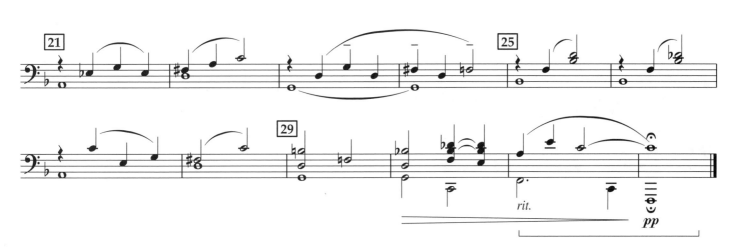

(There's No Place Like)
Home for the Holidays

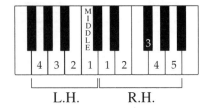

Words by Al Stillman
Music by Robert Allen

Moderately

Oh, there's no place like home for the hol - i - days _____ 'cause no mat - ter how far a -way you roam, _____ when you pine for the

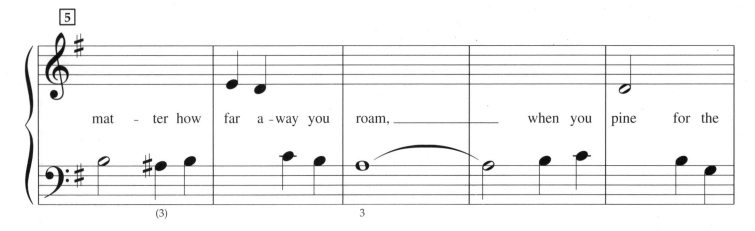

Duet Part (Student plays one octave higher than written.)

Moderately

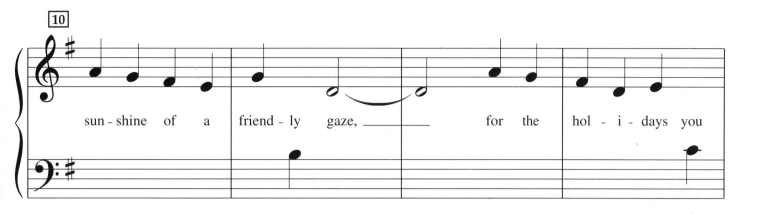

sun - shine of a friend - ly gaze, _____ for the hol - i - days you

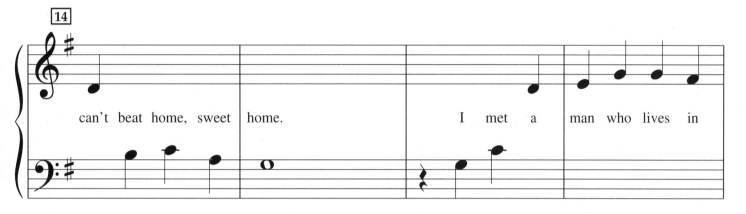

can't beat home, sweet home. I met a man who lives in

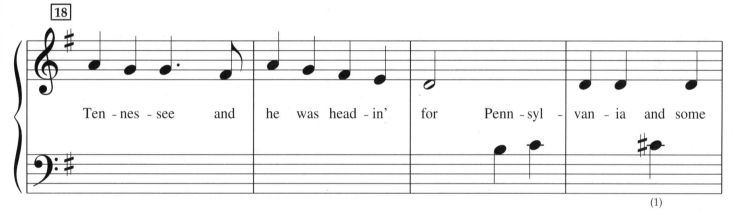

Ten - nes - see and he was head - in' for Penn - syl - van - ia and some

(1)

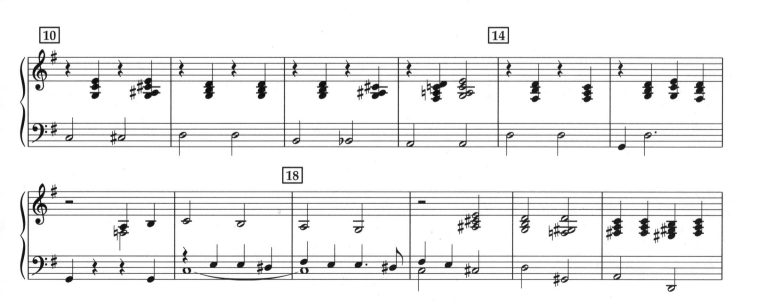

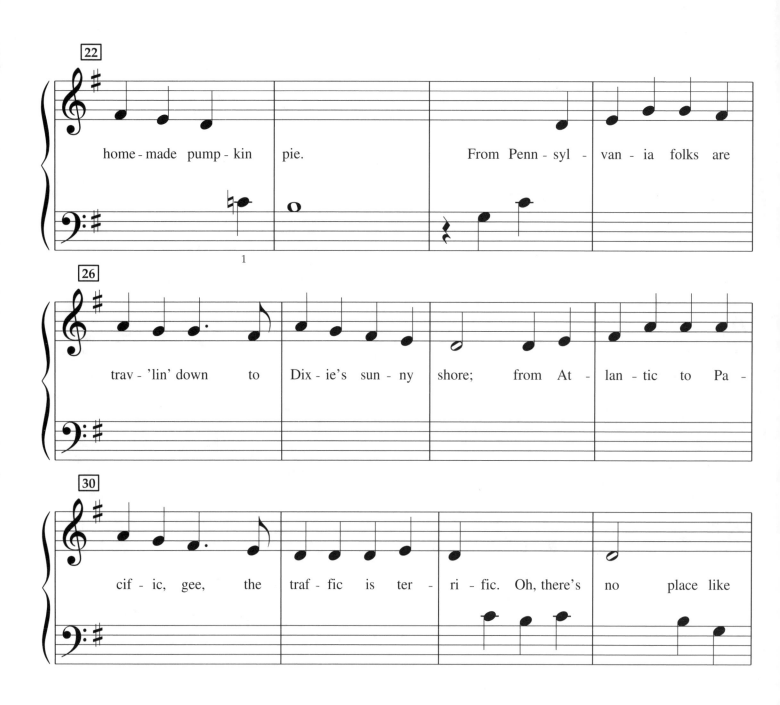

home   for the   hol - i - days _____   'cause no   mat – ter how   far a - way you

(3)

roam, _____   if you   want   to be   hap - py   in a   mil - lion ways, __

_____ for the   hol - i - days you   can't beat home, sweet   home. _____

I Saw Mommy Kissing Santa Claus

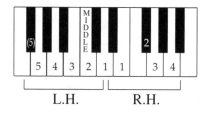

Words and Music by
Tommie Connor

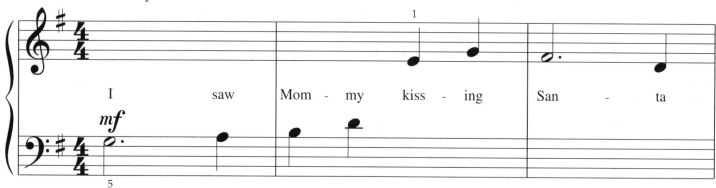

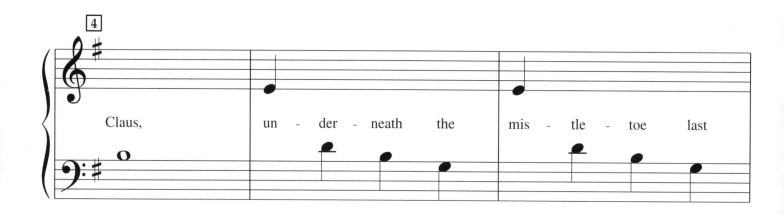

Duet Part (Student plays one octave higher than written.)

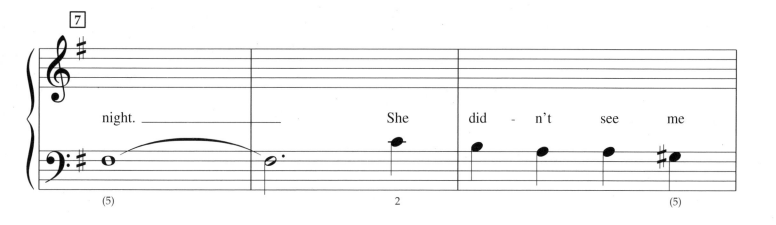

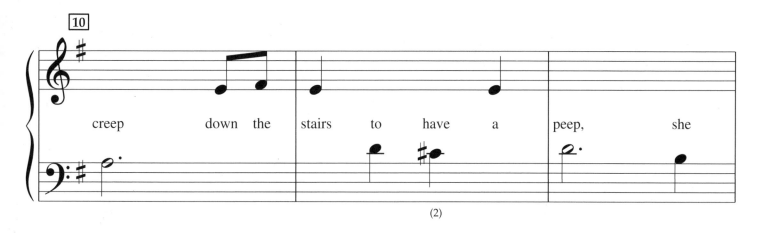

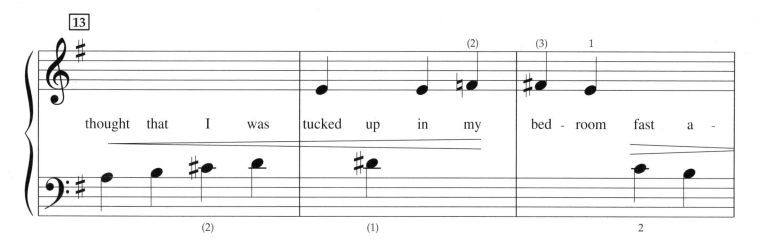

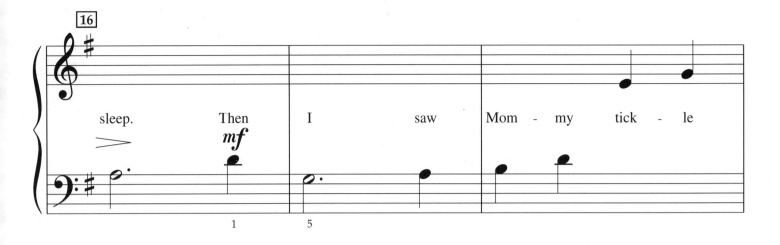

sleep. Then I saw Mom - my tick - le

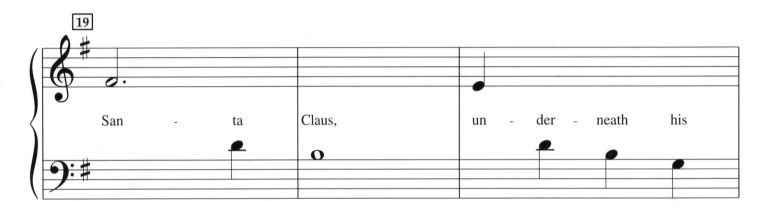

San - ta Claus, un - der - neath his

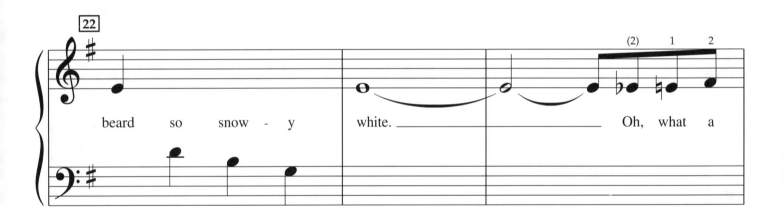

beard so snow - y white. _____ Oh, what a

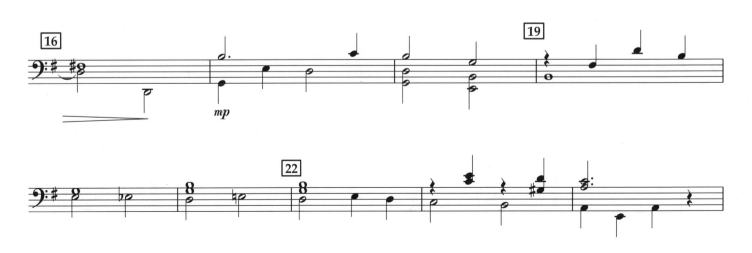

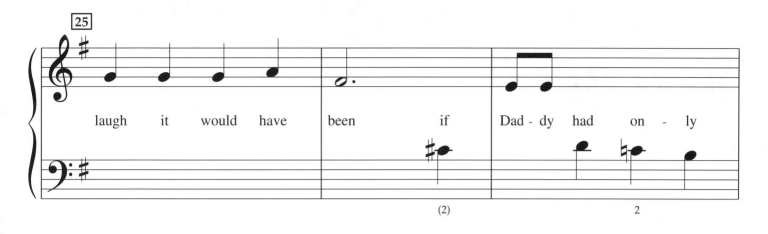

laugh it would have been if Dad - dy had on - ly

seen Mom - my kiss - ing San - ta

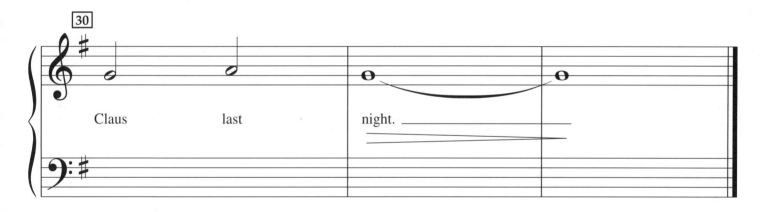

Claus last night. ____

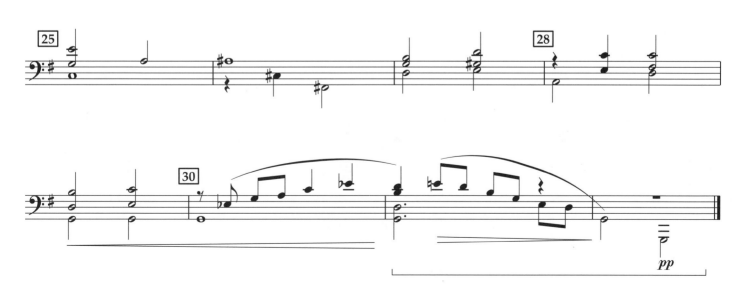

Let It Snow! Let It Snow! Let It Snow!

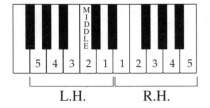

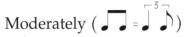

Words by Sammy Cahn
Music by Jule Styne

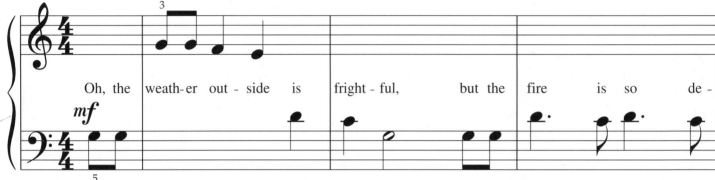

Duet Part (Student plays one octave higher than written.)

snow! It does-n't show signs of stop-ping, and I brought some corn for

pop-ping. The lights are turned way down low; let it snow! let it snow! let it

snow! When we fi-nal-ly kiss good-night, how I'll hate go-ing out in the

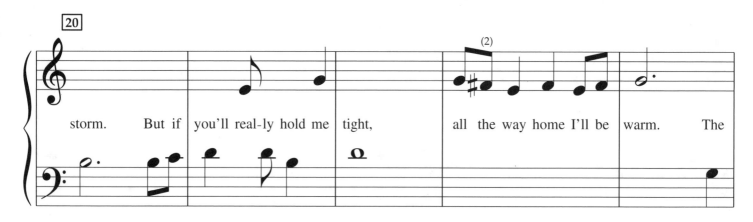

storm.   But if   you'll real-ly hold me   tight,   all   the way home I'll be   warm.   The

fire   is   slow - ly   dy - ing,   and my   dear,   we're still   good - bye - ing,   but as

long   as you love   me   so,   let   it   snow! let   it   snow! let   it   snow!

Mister Santa

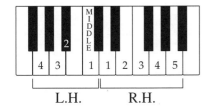

Words and Music by
Pat Ballard

Brightly

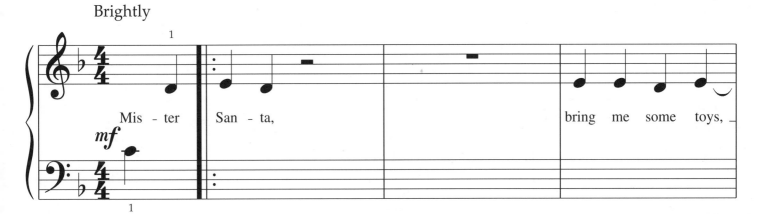

Mis - ter San - ta,   bring me some toys,

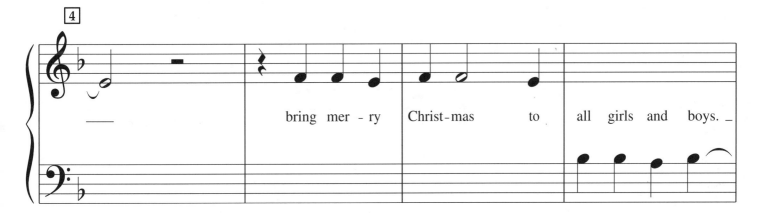

bring mer - ry Christ-mas to all girls and boys.

Duet Part (Student plays one octave higher than written.)

Brightly

And ev - 'ry night I'll go to sleep sing -

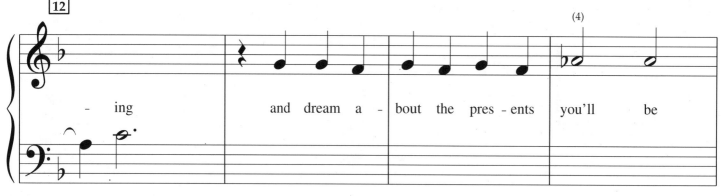

- ing and dream a - bout the pres - ents you'll be

bring - ing. San - ta, prom - ise me, please;

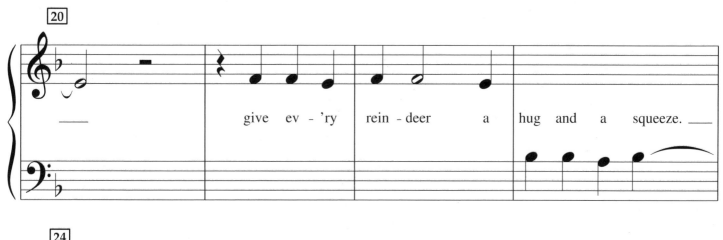

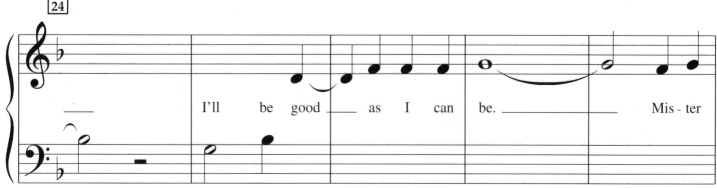

My Favorite Things
from THE SOUND OF MUSIC

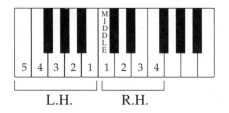

Lyrics by Oscar Hammerstein II
Music by Richard Rodgers

Moderately fast

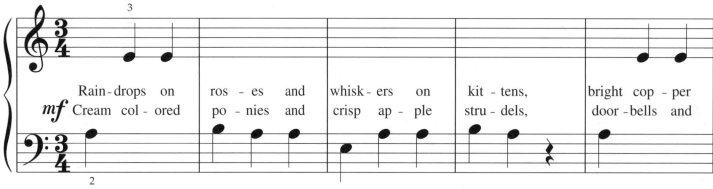

Rain-drops on ros - es and whisk-ers on kit - tens,
bright cop - per
Cream col - ored po - nies and crisp ap - ple stru - dels,
door - bells and

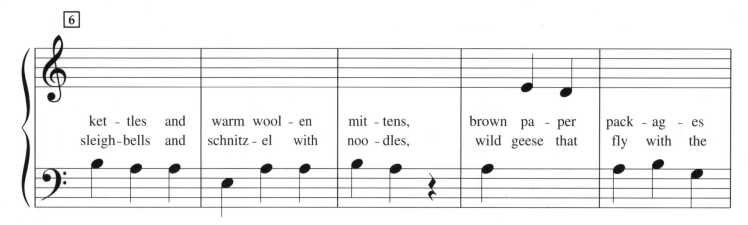

ket - tles and warm wool - en mit - tens, brown pa - per pack - ag - es
sleigh - bells and schnitz - el with noo - dles, wild geese that fly with the

Duet Part (Student plays one octave higher than written.)

Moderately fast

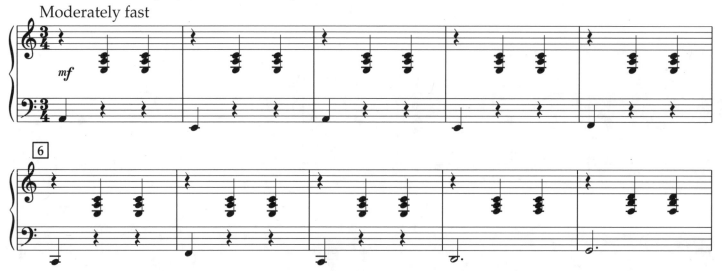

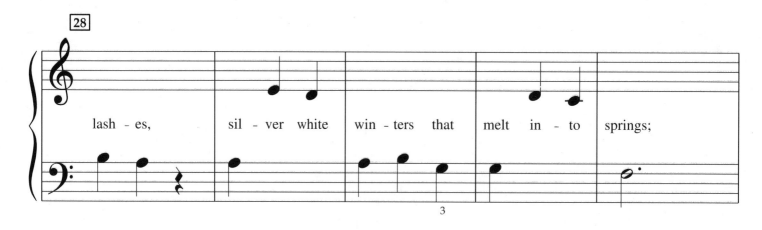

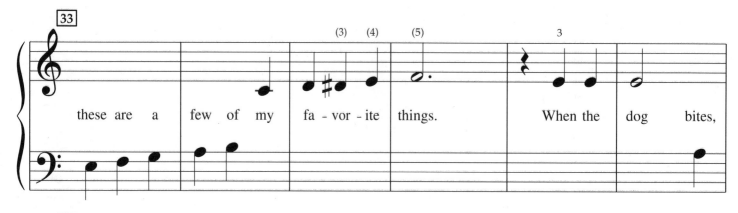

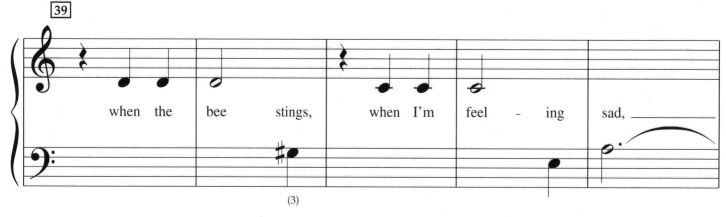

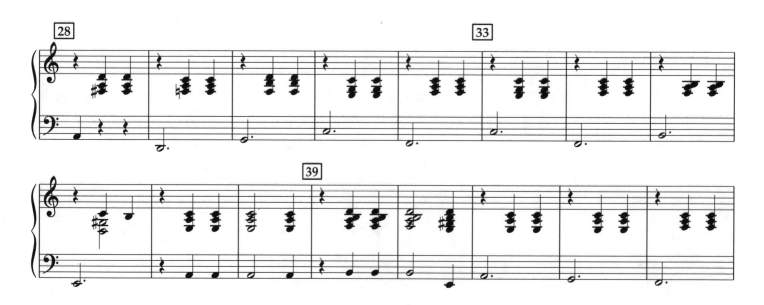

I simply re - mem - ber my fa - vor - ite things and

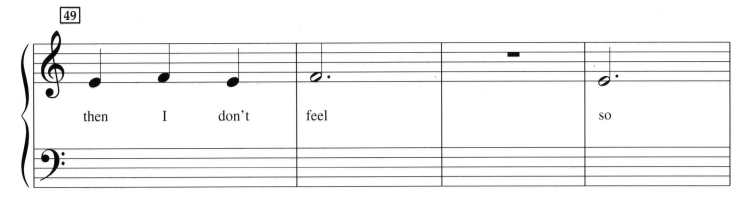

then I don't feel so

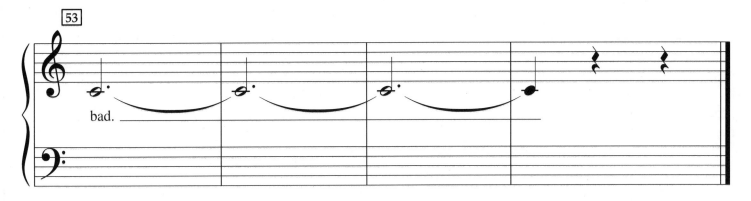

bad. _____

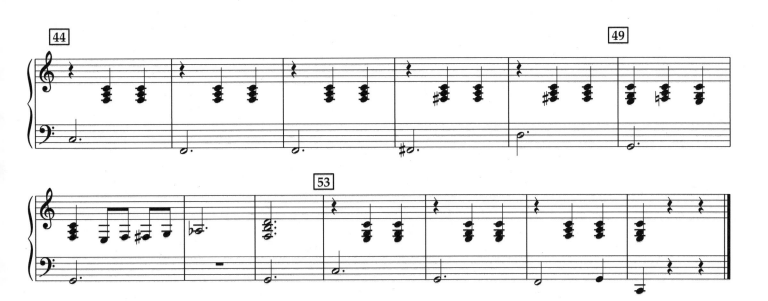

White Christmas
from the Motion Picture Irving Berlin's HOLIDAY INN

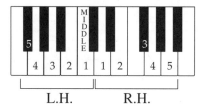

Words and Music by
Irving Berlin

Moderately

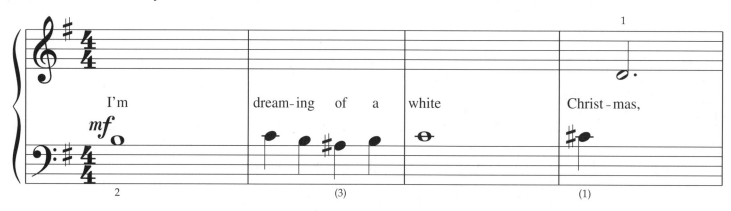

I'm dream-ing of a white Christ-mas,

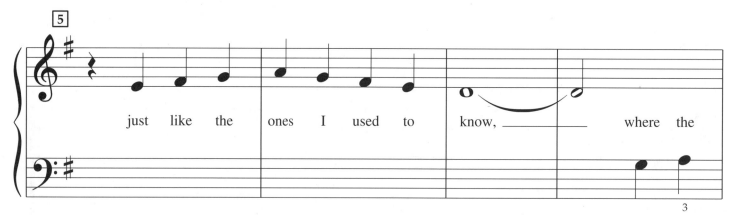

just like the ones I used to know, _____ where the

Duet Part (Student plays one octave higher than written.)
Moderately

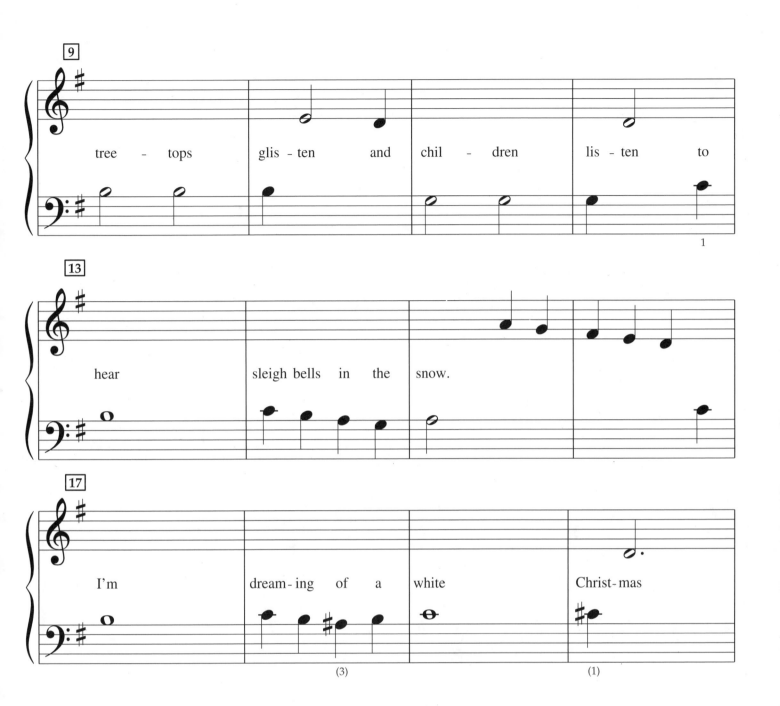

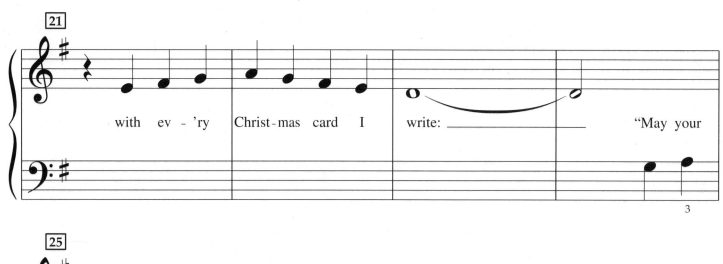

with ev-'ry Christ-mas card I write: _____ "May your

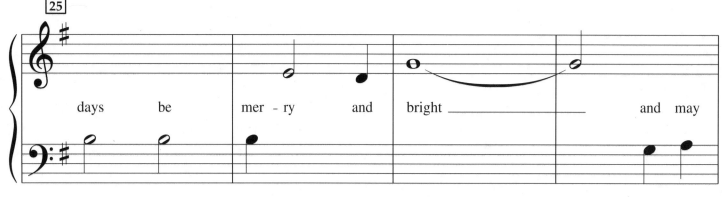

days be mer-ry and bright _____ and may

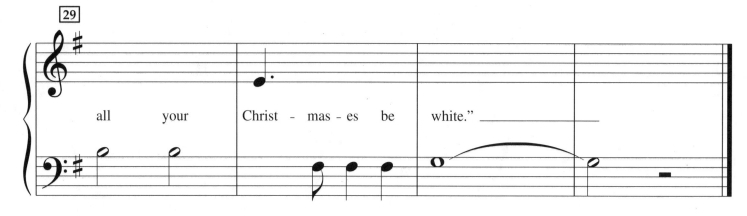

all your Christ-mas-es be white." _____

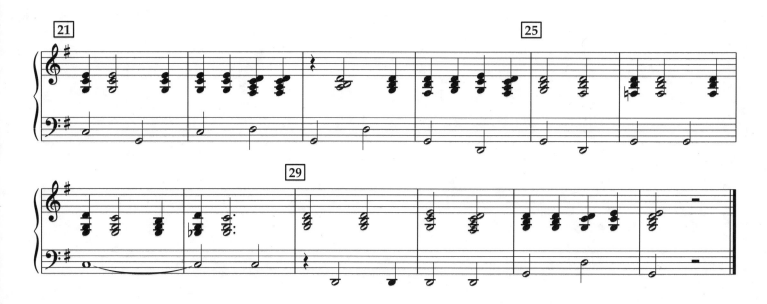